Working Progress, Working Title

JOHN MATTHIAS was born in 1941 in Columbus, Ohio. He has been a Visiting Fellow in poetry at Clare Hall, Cambridge, and lived for much of the 70s and 80s in East Anglia. He teaches at the University of Notre Dame. Matthias's recent books include *A Gathering of Ways* (1991), *Swimming at Midnight: Selected Shorter Poems* (1995), *Beltane at Aphelion: Longer Poems* (1995), and *Pages: New Poems and Cuttings* (2000). In 1998 Robert Archambeau edited *Word Play Place: Essays on the Poetry of John Matthias*.

Working Progress, Working Title

John Matthias

PUBLISHED BY SALT PUBLISHING
PO Box 202, Applecross, Western Australia 6153
PO Box 937, Great Wilbraham, Cambridge PDO CB1 5JX United Kingdom

First published 2002

Printed and bound in the United Kingdom by Lightning Source

Typeset in Swift 9.5 / 13

ISBN 1 876857 41 2 paperback

SP

1 3 5 7 9 8 6 4 2

Contents

Acknowledgements

Swallow Press/Ohio University press for "Pages: From a Book of Years" from John Matthias's American collection, *Pages*, Swallow Press, 2001.

Artists Rights Society for the photograph of Fernand Leger standing in his set design for L'Herbier's film *L'Inhumaine*, and for Francis Picabia's "Fille nee sans mere" © 2001 Artists Rights Society (ARS), New York/ADAGP, Paris.

G. Schirmer Rental and Performance for MIDI keyboard and pianola configurations and click track:
http://www.schirmer.com/balletmec/06.html

Roy George and Associates, Studio portrait of Hedy Lamarr.

Automystifstical Plaice

In the beginning
without any mother the girl was born a machine.
In the year of erotic parades.
The Novia poured out the oil the gears were engaged
the études composed and the light bulb
was Amèricaine. Voilà Picabia sweetheart of first
occupation voilà ballet mécanique.
We'll not eat our bread by the sweat of our brows
in the end: Je viens pour toujours
it is error and grief you'll be known by
the strength of our steel
the number of rivets and not by the river
where fishermen cast or the last
of your towers to build on the strength of our dowry.
Antheil Olga Boski Hedy and Ez, she says:
Or probably better
Olga and Ez, Antheil and Boski [Hedy Keisler Mandl Lamarr.
That's Mandl, Fritz, from Vienna, the armaments man,
the war profiteer. Hedy Keisler, the naked broad in the film.
It won't be a dance, it won't be ballet mécanique.

Ecstasy, rather, a run through the woods and a swim.
The actress saying: sex in this movie is real,
Mandl's lieutenants will buy up & burn any print they can find
so Hedy and Fritz can entertain Hitler and Mus.
Aribert Mog is displaced; the telescope on the lens
enlarges another face
from about a decade before.]

 They enter a judgment,
Théâtre des Champs Elysées. Everyone's there. The soloist
doesn't know that he is a she. He doesn't know
he's set up, doesn't yet know they've scripted him in a riot
(those lights are too many, too bright.)
Mere human being he sits there robotic she looks like
a presence out of Bohemia via Berlin's RUR.
He begins with Sonata Sauvage.
A camera's panning the audience, picks out the famous:
Picasso and Joyce, Duchamp, Milhaud and Satie.
We see them there with Leblanc as Lescot in the film
but we don't hear a sound Mr. Pound leaping
right out of his seat and shaking a fist as people begin
to walk out on Antheil himself at his Airplane Sonata
by now and sweating away but we don't hear a thing as we gaze
at the girl without any mother born a machine
who would sing out succès du scandale a clickityclack
of the dactylicanapests jerking the film
through a circle of light the soloist booed from the stage
the piano rolls looping their loops
in twelve pianolas electronic bells and a xylophone siren
another Picabia made from the parts
of a Model-T Ford.

                    Good Lord, she says, Mon Dieu.
That must have been one nine two three, the year I went
to the races with Hem at Anteuil, the year
young Antheil was going to play Cyclops for Jim.
A working title indeed, she says, a walking tittle or tattle I'd say
to your automystiftistical plaice—
you're fishing again in some pre-Riemannian river
and don't understand the riveters have it all over
the rhetors who can't even master the minor recursions
while minding the algorithmical gaps.
No one could actually *play* that piano roll A wrote into the score,
the digitals moving at speeds and at intervals
nobody's ten carboniferous digits could match.
So down at the hurdle went Manzu, tossing his jock,
and Héros the Twelfth and L'Yser dashed at long odds
for the finish. Seining out in the sea near Le Havre
you wouldn't net any sonnets much less Seigneurs
out of Proust. You understand, she insists,
there *are* no parallel lines in rivers that wind & nothing but
        nothing
my love appears to cohere from *inside* the system
trust *me* I'm a truffler I *know* my way around.

And Pound once again that very same year in his Treatise?
claiming for A's diachronic harmonics
that sounds whatever the pitch combination etcetera
harmonize across time
these series of chords these arpeggios wait to embrace
through an interval
                                        silence
the crux of the thing
the space in the music like space in some canvas
by Lewis his fine demarcations of volume,
cylindrical forms: You do comprehend these recursions are
        different
from those you'd expect,
the power plant cycles like no minuet?

                                        & so A, she says,
was the cause of that riot but nowhere was seen
in the film. It's me, it is I, on the screen!
They call me there the austere Mademoiselle Claire Lescot.
I'm some kind of cubist cold fish, the girl
without any mother born a machine who can nonetheless sing
and I stare down those rioting plebs at the Champs Elysées
alive in the interval A absconditus diminished
however you like. [81: chez vous. Demain à sept heures.
82: musique imprévue. 83: odieuse, odieuse. 84: atmosphère
torturante quand elle laisse enfin percer le secret . . .
son immense douleur inhumaine . . .
85, 86, 87: In reel time
we're counting the titles, we number the causes, effects:
Sonata Sauvage, piano, piano roll, siren
and dactyl and drum.
Will George in the war be faithful
to Boski his wife? Will Olga or Ez trumpet Mus?
Will young Fräulein Keisler run naked as Hedy Lamarr?
Fishing or fasting, reprogram, reverse it
and search]

Your working title, she says,
might as well gesture at Czech. The Gödels and Capeks fished
for me in my motherless maze when I thought I was
Daumier's laundress and not Miss Sullarobotess,
some loopy machine in your ghost,
the ganef your ganglia somehow encoded, the chip on your
    shoulder,
the quantum mechanic under the hood of your truck.
Before they made me the knee of your curve, the neural pathway
encrypted for good. Was I not to dissolve in *I am*
but as antiparticulate anapest?
And that other, doctor, a dactyl, or a catcall out of the pit.
Anyway the joke was on P: A's pianola replacing
the Sapphics & he himself its antistrophe, turns unrolling
Daphne's thighs from the bark.

So Model-T begat Picabia who as machinist made the shape that named a choreography. And then Antheil's recital drove the riot L'Herbier required for Lescot before she visits Léger's laboratory where her lover there among the angles and the geometric shapes, the silver disks and metal rods and knobs and dials and flashing beams of light, transfigures her. [Hedwig Keisler's in Vienna at that moment and she's eight years old. She's also in the lab. She's in the music and the dance and the machine.] And then when A has finished playing at that theater and gifting us with such an angry crowd in *L'Inhumaine*, he synchronizes those piano rolls whose loops and variants of eighty-eight prefigure microsecond hops between the frequencies of anti-jamming programs in torpedoes or computer links or cordless phones. This is Ballet Mécanique: the draft. This the working title. This the initial location, the automys-tifstical plaice. We don't hear a thing as we call up Archival Search: Were you, Oh My Baby, meant to walk that washer woman up the stairs with Léger-Daumier? The print went to Vienna and premiered in silence, running credits anyway for Synchronisme Musicale. The ostinati rolled for friends and patrons five days later at the Salle Pleyel.

If first the vertical and then the horizontal penetrations were deriv-atives of pianist and pianola, neither got it all entirely right, though both had caught a ride on George's rickshaw. Our guest was still a ghost, the cyborg wasn't yet a sibyl on the line. And A himself could never fully realize his 1923 designs. His codes were still dependent on a vacuum force and paper rolls with which he sought to synchronize his twelve or more machines. He hadn't met the Midi, technical cousin of Claire, his digital and instrumental interface. As if you'd teach the retrofitted to respond in synch, but not for sixty years. Still, the lady out of Daumier walks up the stairs and up the stairs and up the stairs once more in *Ballet Mécanique* the film. If Claire Lescot stood in for one piano, these stone steps beside the Seine and these looped thirty frames appear and reap-pear to summon music no one hears where tie-rods, pistons, wheels and gears and abstract forms reflected in the steel of a pris-matic fracturing all gleam and try to sing.

E	03:10	E	02:38
F	04:01	F	03:20
G	06:11	G	05:09
H	06:40	H	05:33
I	07:01	I	05:51
J	08:05	J	06:54
K	11:20	K	09:26
L	11:32	L	09:37
M	11:59	M	09:59
N	13:02	N	10:52
O	13:39	O	11:22
P	14:40	P	12:14
Q	16:32	Q	13:47
R	18:51	R	15:42
S	21:35	S	17:59
T	22:05	T	18:24
U	23:05	U	19:14
V	23:16	V	19:24
X	23:47	X	19:49
Y	24:29	Y	20:24
Z	24:50	Z	20:42
AA	26:00	AA	21:40
BB	30:03	BB	25:02

Says Ezra Pound: EP. He plays. All gleam and try to sing. And then Léger: Léger. Says George Antheil: Anteuil. That piece in place. Police will net you rioters at any cybernetic database. Then peace. Or flounder there. All champs, these guys. All champs Champs Elysées. If someone might just reconnect. That wire. That Novia who pours out oil, those gears that re-engage. Say P & A: Machines are musical. Machines are part of life. It's right that one should feel a little warm. One does so feel. Or cold. It's not required of anyone to kneel. When they tried to integrate the music and the film they didn't mesh. They went their separate ways as separate works like two berserks in RUR or Léger's lab. In 1923 the pianolas were all out of synch. You've said. But now the Midi in her Quadra form's all smiles. Disklavier by Yamaha. [As if you'd count out miles of spectrum spreads with Miss Lamarr.] At some café-tabac you'd linger over a petit vin blanc or modify the track at will and run the thing right back. And was that laundress's one friend a fisherman?

Oh yes. In all the winding rivers and at sea. Says he:

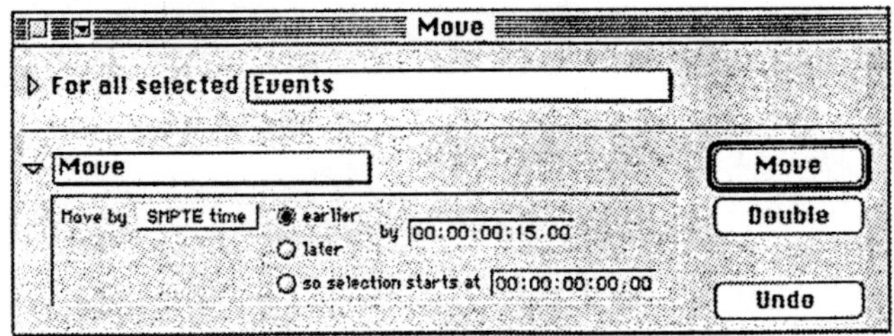

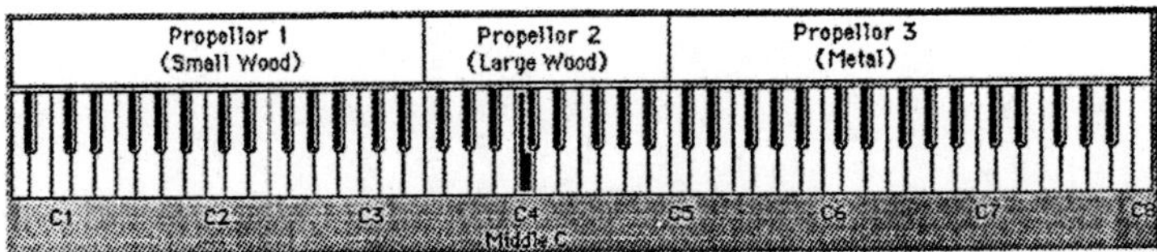

EP:

Not Ezra Pound: Express Pâquette (in negligée).

Not George Antheil: Anteuil. No not Champs Elysées.

In prose: Who goes? The ghost of Claire Lescot.

And not Lescot: Sans mother a machine.

A hemistich? A click. Some dream you've seen.

Some obligation anyway to start assigning parts. Whose art?

Not mine. Some rhyme or other you'd suppose.

Delete suppose: Some interlude between the creatures' double
    features.

Lescot escorted from the stage. What page?

Léger: Constructed objects. Fountain pen. A pendulum against a
   silhouette.

Antheil: A cigarette?

[Lamarr: Pâquette!]

Léger: These squares and circles, animation: play.

EP: I see arpeggios. Prismatic images of day.

Picabia: The Lady Light Parisienne, a glow.

[Lamarr, Pâquette: Lescot!]

Antheil: They said I had all Paris by the ear; I was in full career.

Léger: That year I had them by . . .

[Pâquette: I know, the eye!]

Picabia: By Model-T or Model-A, I had divined a rod.

Léger: My god, these quotes: A shiny metal sphere.

Antheil: That spins and disappears.

[Lamarr: For what?]

Antheil: A thought

emerging intermittently between the wars among the whores of
discourse. [Horse, that is, of race course. Force of different color?
Go.
System error 218: Anteuil

not Antheil.
Astound not Ezra Pound.
Constructed objects, fountain pen, a pendulum against a
silhouette. Hedy Keisler
growing up: New file]

                        Which says, my Sister System,
I'll not take it back. I'll just
stay on track I think and tell you one more time
it's prisms and not prison like I said.
I didn't say? Well, anyway.
And no dissolves or fade-outs, no irises or wipes,
everything quick-cut and edgy from
the pure geometries to Kiki's painted lips & eyes.
I loved that walk from *L'Inhumaine* right up and into Dudley
        Murphy's
lens where only I in that ballet was
fully conscious. I even heard the absent music in my ears.
They'd added something by Milhaud of course, but secretly
I walked those stairs on George's arm,
our loops and our recursions not quite waltzing to Matilda
right in step, it's true. Then suddenly for me
no more Champs Elysées.
No more long afternoons with Hem out at Anteuil or
drinks at the Café du Dome. Ah, home:
My favorite place, my resting plaice, Mon Vieux!
Who'd have programmed metamorphoses
like these: migraines among transmigrating neural forms
and even A
in Hollywood at work on *Plainsman*
for De Mille and Paramount. They tied up Gary Cooper
to a stake & lit the fire beneath his feet accompanied
by something like the Mechanisms for piano
that had conjured rioters for Claire Lescot when I was she.

The silent Diva and the Model-T get scrapped when even Dali
comes to town proclaiming Cecil B a great Surrealist.
The times are strange. Air waves all awash with bands that swing
or Autrey singing down home out of range.
Ecstasy had made a star Miss Lamarr although nobody
in the USA had seen it. [Girl seventeen & born
of mother no machine. Alas, an unfucked bride: Swimming
          naked
and observed by handsome virile male actor name of Mog,
her simulated sex on sofa later advertised to be
the real ride. Movements to be reproduced by analog
or digitize? First prize. Alu will occur
three hundred thousand times in human genome
to be known and coded soon enough.
That's why A and Dali loose their dog the Andalou
on B and you]

Coeval, then, & coefficient in the codices
of coinage, they sit together
in the private screening room: the mogul
and the moilers make a single molecule for a moment
as modalities come into play: The way
the young man strops his razor by a balcony, then deliberately
draws the blade across the woman's open eye that bleeds
on down the screen where just before they'd lit up
the Dakotas with some rushes of Calamity
and Wild Bill to test the sound. No sound now but
Dali's voice, whispering to George and Miss Lamarr,
De Mille beginning to be ill:
                                In '29 we used a Gramophone
behind a curtain: *Tristan* and some tangos,
but you'll get the dirty puns: That man who cuts her eye
first glances at la lune and then we see her
face as if it were her ass, his gaze half-mooned,
her eye become her oeil du cul he'd diddle with a dildoe
so we play this little coup de vache
on every scatalogue and watch the ants emerge
from his stigmata, no? the way he's roped
to this machinery he drags, pianos stuffed with putrefying
donkeys and dos padres, si? the priests tied up and
on their backs in bondage of some kind as part of this
contrivance & De Mille out of his seat by now
and saying brother rat [?] or bugger that [? the file at
this point labeled diction inconsistent] so
we'll give them Custer Lincoln Hickok Cody Hopalong
and Jesus Christ at Rancho Grande, George
but what the hell is this?

                    I don't know, she says,
but that's the way I heard it. Also, I'd begun
of late to feel odd affinities with Paramount and MGM
and fully integrated scores of soothing violins
and mellow horns, and more than that I had this queer
attraction [was I Lesbo? did my database pick up
some viral pixels on my transatlantic trek?] for Miss Lamarr.
Although I still missed Paris & Picabia & Ez,
I'd always been, just like they said, Amèricaine: as Novia
or light bulb or arpeggio or pitch. I'd harmonized
across the times as if embracing intervals in rhymes
and here I was with Salvador and
Cecil's kitsch, my former lover back there fishing off
Le Havre and my senescent self
still climbing stairs in ludic loops. [42: Keyboard
and the bleeding head of donkey A.
43: Donkey A replaced by donkey B. 44: Male cyclist
in a housemaid's dress, a closing door.
45: A woman's wagging tongue whose text
is next: Tirer la langue;
it reels in time, those white keys teeth, the language
flowing through a leaking roof
a gamble & a Gödel proof; donkey C
is in our key, alive
alert, aloof.]

She says, although I seemed to be that
one qui perd ses dents and only climbed
the stairs, I felt immortal next to Hedy now who really
lived and so could only die, her dark machine
in that bright ghost a spectrum spread
like some black raven's wing. And George would write
their song. But as for you, my neuralnetted friend,
no one nominates an end, so try again at the beginning
where you counted rivets and were tempted
by the tempered steel. I'd style you as titular
Titanothere, cloned from Eocene into titanium,
statistical as your specific gravity
& valence & atomic weight. If you could swim
they'd cast you in her place.

In the Salzburg palace basement or the hidden conference room of his Vienna flat, he'd show himself another print of the offending scene of that same film his agents had again obtained at great expense—and then destroy it. Obsession made him a discerning connoisseur; this print just a little faded, that one slightly dark. But always there was her orgasmic St. Teresa-of-a-mouth à la Bernini and Delilah nipples that De Mille would say were sugar-coated with religion just for Samson's tongue. And writhing hips and thighs. And naked ass. Of course she'd left him—actually escaped by means of a disguise and complicated ruse—sometime in the spring of 1937. But she'd listened first to all those conversations among guests who'd come on business with the Hertzenberger Industries. Like Krupp and Basil Zaharov, Mandl had the reputation of a man who'd start a war if that would move the goods. Goebbels kissed her hand from time to time and Göring held her chair. No one understood that she could understand the technicalities. It was all a kind of music that accompanied the movie in her mind. As if someone who sat beside her at the baby grand on which she'd conjured storms in *Ecstasy* kept pointing out a spectral figure at an upright in the corner shadows of the stately palace room where she had been a silent party to analyses of radio control and interception by the politicians and the engineers. As if he played a phrase, a bar, a whole ballet of permutations that configured variations on the number eighty-eight and all were answered by the keys before her note for note. As if the notes were hopping frequencies no jealous husband lurking on a narrow signal band could jump or jam or even chase pursuant to an instrument for her arrest, and she could send encryptions of her own desires to a satellite or submarine in some determinable future's sky or sea. As if she were herself some wireless net through which transmission played its working titles and entitled wakings and its wacky tales, through which some Claire Lescot prepared to solo for her Turing test or sing along like yet another pianola at the prom.

Was it impractical to play piano rolls inside the missiles and torpe-
does that a radio would guide along a band of frequencies stretch-
ing out to eighty-eight? Although this music from phantasmagoric
Paris earned a US patent for its military application and eventually
produced more racket than a dozen riots at Théâtre des Champs
Elysées, in 1941 the War Department didn't think that George and
Hedy could defeat the Nazis on their own. They thought they
could. Leaving Cecil B and Dali talking teleology at Paramount,
they went to work and made a template down at Hedy's place
outside LA at canyon Benedict. In 1957 the transistors at Sylvania
finally made it sing. And now your cell phone rings. The wireless
internet turns up a site devoted altogether to the Midi programs
and the bank of synthesizers and the Apple Quadra that have
synchronized the very music that created hopping frequencies and
play it dancing à la ballet mécanique across contemporary spec-
tra spread out in the night. Claire Lescot again walks shaken from
the stage. Léger's laundress climbs and climbs the stairs. Milstar
system's crosslink disk antennae make secure a constellation that's
controlled by downlinked signals playing their encryptions which
have harmonized in time.

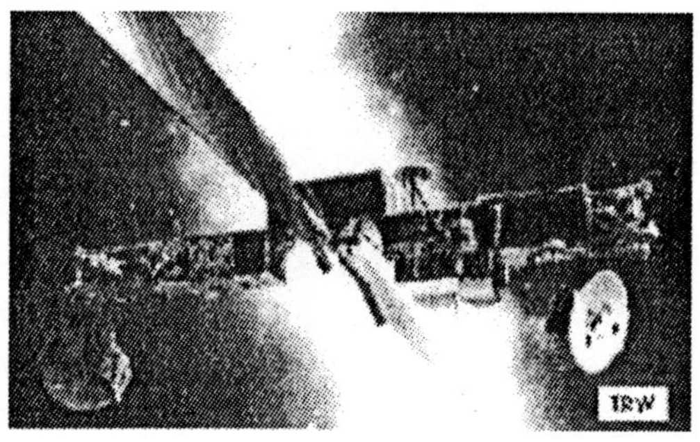

If EP thumped a drum in Paris and attempted a bassoon when A composed his trios and sonatas there for Olga Rudge, Harpo Marx in Hollywood was B flat major clarinetist in the symphonietta thrown together by despairing exiles, studio composers and indigenous eccentrics just to play a bit of Schoenberg in the war and keep their spirits up. It somehow follows thus. And A imagines all of them quite disembodied in a beautiful machine. With other incompatibles. Where into some blind switchman's roundhouse puffs an insubstantial 1850s Difference Engine pulling phantom coaches from the past all loaded with the numbers meaning Novia and étude and Américaine multiplied by the idea of a red caboose. Where EP is Express Pâquette. Who plays, that whore, for larks. That open door of Montparnasse. And Harpo Marx: These sparks that fly. And A's pneumatic-driven notes become electric quotes from 1923. In 1941 it's done in spite of Paramount for Miss Lamarr. And then it's done for Milstar in the sky or Disklavier that's clear on time's uncertain rhymes. Twelve hundred measures in your file for sequencing. Select your samples from a hand-cranked siren and orchestral bell and biwing props. Prepare a click track and beware the signatures that change six hundred times. Calculate in milliseconds and deploy the sixteen retrofitted grands. Clap hands. Enter isomorphic. Admit the Laundress and delete Lescot. Delete the autological. Let go. When every patron on the lam cries out: just one more time, and play it Sam, the answer sticks right in your gorge: I am not Sam, my name is George.

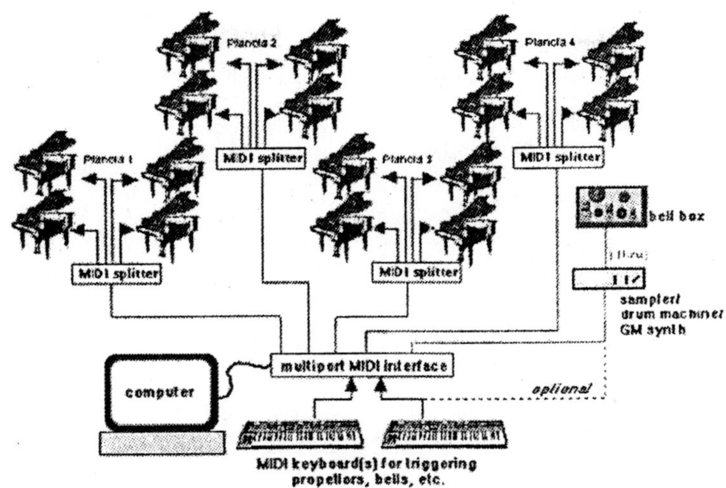

Not C. De Mille. An illness in the village of the will.

A poisoned well? A ringing bell.

Disgust, disgrace. With nearly everything in place.

In Hollywood is nothing good. The marble temples made of
    wood.

The templates, too. The idol Dagon stuck in glue.

A certain bet & neural net? The Russell paradox inside your set.

A rural ease and honey bees. Returning money on the lease.

CB: Your friends were all effete.

Antheil: This film of yours about Lafitte!

They fucked each other in the ass.

[And on the grass, those pirate lads.]

[Lescot: Our Hem went running with the bulls]

CB: Could any of them pay their bills?

Lamarr: I've nipples here to sell.

Antheil: And they had stories they could tell.

CB: Who's this Lescot? I'm sure not anyone I know.

Lafitte: A pirate! Get that in your notes.

Bassoon: Put "Harpo Marx" in quotes.

EP: When he was young, George worked for me.

We're stuck here in this DVD. Desktop, laptop, box of chips.

Mainframe swallows up our fame.

Bits of code all recombined. The Seine might just as well be
        Rhine.

CB: The past. Antheil: At last.

Lamarr: Too long is late but not too far.

Plaintext cyphered: stare by star

says steer [does it] by stair? Milhaud's prime beef qui était sur le
toit is either going up
or coming down whenever knot is now
is notnow not-knot anyhow old Mac iron bomb [ap-
pended copy to a copy and said *copy that*
repeats itself

plus copy of that copy &
original all hypercarded glut or metalepsis
boot again you fruit: It's Nipples
not In Naples.
Lafitte not With Your Feet.
Buccaneer, a bayou waterway, a privateer, one hundred twenty-
          three
pirogues & Andy Jackson too: New score]

                                        She says,
& that was Limbo not That Bimbo, Tex.
Try Lingo next: try glossing alu, angel capital, AI and ASR.
Try haptic interface and PGP and Qu-bit. Luddite
if you like but total touch environment is on the way with
virtual sex, though Hedy gets the parts in all these films.
As for me, I ended up at MIT in some robotics lab,
but that comes later on. In between comes Friedman cracking
        Purple
and Los Alamos and CB's pirate flick with George's score
and yes my own dear sweet dumb ex out riding
on his charger from Anteuil brandishing his relic of a saber
from the Franco-Prussian war and straight
into a column of advancing German tanks.
Never underestimate the new technologies. The plaice
is in your face. Strange to think CB had made
his first *Commandments* in the very year of *L'Inhumaine*.
The rest, perhaps, amendments,
and some justice there in Dali's deli east of the Chinese.
On Murok Sands in the Mojave
Ramses & 300 chariots a Golden Calf the Laws & Orgies
all the Israelites the Pharaoh's city and an avenue
of twenty sphinxes worked out the techniques to blast
the Paris avant-garde and put the Samson-shears
in Hedy's hand. All downhill for Paris. Everybody in LA.
Sell out or be sold into some exhibition of degenerates;
collaborate and sing like Edith Piaf
or the Chevalier.

They told me *she* was working on
Tortilla Flats and just broke down completely when the news
came in about the war. The journey over on the Normandie
with Louis Mayer, who had offered her a job, and old
Cole Porter who kept whispering *oh you're the top* and
it's delovely and *experiment* right in her ear
had made her pretty optimistic in a gray grim world. But on
that day she walked right off the set and right past
Spencer Tracy, Steinbeck and the lot of them still costumed as
that simple little waif from Mexico and saying Find Me
George Antheil. We're going to sink the Hertzenbergers
and the Krupps with my torpedo.
That they tried to do, and for a while I toted round their
template, patented for George and Hedy Keisler Markey
(which was briefly once her married name).

The post-war world was confusing and a little flat
for someone like myself who'd left her husband fishing
off Le Havre to join the brilliant entourage that pitched
its diachronics across time but came to grief in rhyme.
For a girl like me without a mother born as a machine,
I'd always had a mortal fear of *Philistine*. I went
to Princeton first and showed the figures round the Institute
where only the eccentric Barricelli took an interest.
We played four hands at George's early compositions sitting
side by side at one piano. I think he'd seen my film.
He said Your mutant language has evolved by crossings and
selections, just like species do. Take one of my cards.
A symbiogenic birth entirely from the numbers operating
on their own in Simula on DEC Sys 10. But here it is,
product of a B-math symbiont or parasite. Give it to Lamarr.
Your friends' piano-rolling weapon maybe didn't
end the war, but it could end the world. Its progeny will
be evolved in ways you cannot see and you yourself deserve
a Gödel number for your pains. He said Are you alive?
I thought he was a little nuts, but kissed him anyway
before we drove to town for Samson on a local screen....

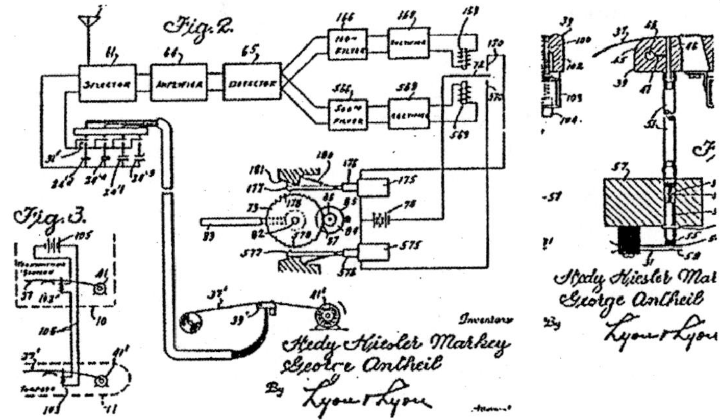

And there she was in all her glory with that hunk
Mature who wielded for sure the jawbone of the ass
against his enemies just like it says in *Judges*.
Judge us, that's what we said in Paris, if you dare!
And did they dare? Did they draft a thousand barbers
just to cut our hair? Who but we could best put forth
the riddle of the lion's carcass and the swarm of bees?
We'd caught three hundred foxes, put the firebrands
to their tails, and loosed them barking in the standing corn.
Such corn there was! And kitsch!
We dwelt then at the top of Etam rock
which crumbled in the end and made us exiles.
Had they done their plowing with our heifer? Did
George's hair grow long again grinding in the prison house
of Paramount? Hedy played the harlot for the Philistines,
but that was all an act . . .

                              I hear they keep
old prints of *L'Inhumaine* and *Ballet Mécanique* in some
dark archive where, like Mandl with his prints of *Ecstasy*,
they turn each other on with clips cut from the body
of our work. At MIT they want to know what makes me tick.
I blip and flicker, but I turn no trick.
They're racing with the Japs at Honda to perfect their
human motion simulation software
and a clumsy biped toddler they call Dick.
I don't tell them much. What floundered first on Flanders Field
wasn't plaice. In any case. Nor when jockeys rode against
the Panzers crossing near Sars-Poteries
the undefended river Meuse. That other river that I loved
still passes Troyes and Melun and our
shining hungry haunted city of Between the Wars before
it loops through Normandy and past Rouen to empty in the sea.
Someone's fishing there. He looks like you.
I think I loved him once.
A washer-woman tired as I am now stops her climbing
up the endless stairs beside the Seine
and looks behind her with appreciation at the view.

Pages

from a book of years

Part One

I

1959. And underneath the photographs
names of people you can count

as if they numbered works and days
and years: one and one by one

become again these Davids, Joels & Fayes
and 1959's about to flower

flame again to 1960, 1961

The flower in the flame. The fame of that. Those days. People you
could count who counted then. David, Joel and Faye; Margaret,
Ann, and Margaret-Ann; Sondra, Bonnie, Lisa, Lennie, Kaye. Luck
(o sister life) you'd think was little more than winning dashes,
listening to the jazz at Marty's 502, kissing Cora with your left
hand up her skirt in that black and battered Studebaker Lark. Boris
Pasternak, I'd say. I'll bet not one of you has read a word by Boris
Pasternak. I didn't mean his novel. Sister Life, I'd say. I loved the
title, hadn't read the poems. My Sister Life. I'd run until I felt like
I could fly, then stand under ice-cold showers for an hour. The
tingle of well-being being well inside the brackets of a decade for
another several months

whose year whose yearbook opens really. On your lap.

Who'd say Nadir How Now Restless Wind or Endine Tim Tam Quil
and Gallant Man what's Bold Ruler Oligarchy Jewel's Reward? If
horses were wishes, what's your wish: To winter in Kentucky,
summer in Saratoga.

Rook-and-queen your combination in a close, coming back against
the dragon variation of a Russian's elegant Sicilian.

Khrushchev in New York. His phrase for the occasion not a quote
you'd look up in a book by Boris P. His rook not named for Tim

Tam, nor his queen for Nadir. In the rulers' table names decline
like sentences beneath the photographs that you could count as
Dave and Joel and Faye: King Saud is sand and Faisal backs to
Franco Gamal Abdel Nasser turns to Eisenhower Pope John Ho Chi-
minh

David Goss and Pham Van-dong
Joel & Bonnie

Margaret, Ann, and Margaret-Ann
One & one by one

in time you do forget well almost all of it the whole damn thing
goes almost blank

goes wholly blank in time

for Governor-General Viscount Charles John Lyttelton Cobham, say.

II

Disasters 1959: Rio de Janeiro plane crash
Guadalajara bus and train Formosa

earthquake Istanbul a fire Western
Pakistan a flood & in the Persian Gulf typhoons

a caved-in mine in Merlebach and just
northeast of Newfoundland a sunken ship,

Blue Wave

I put my hand directly up her skirt and she did not say no don't
do it didn't say a thing and so I kept it there a moment just above
the knee and then began advancing slowly with my finger tips in
little steps

blue wave, blue wave

And out there somewhere Viscount Charles John Lyttelton
Cobham.

This year Raymond Chandler died and so did Abbott's friend
Costello. It's hard to think of Abbott all alone his eyes upon
Costello's derby hanging on the hatrack in the hall. For days you
keened in grief for Errol Flynn your only child's Robin. General
Marshall, Admiral William Halsey also on the list. And Ike in tears.
Who'd say weep my love for

John Foster Dulles
Amy's mother Florence Smith

For every day there's death you've
got to chronicle and someone writes the years in yearbooks puts
eventually the volumes in a right and goodly order on the shelf

who loved her best friend Amy's mother Florence Smith.

Joel and I would play this game called Scrounge. Others I've discovered called it Bernie-Bernie. You could lose a lot of money and a number of our friends and victims did. After dropping all his cash one night Carl Butler put his watch into the pot and then his shoes. Who the hell would want your shoes said Joel. They're first-rate shoes said Carl. They're ordinary Keds said Joel so what's about them so first-rate. Anyway he lost these too and then he went home barefoot. The music that we listened to was jazz: Monk and Miles, the MJQ, Dave Brubeck. It all seemed so subversive. We'd smoke, play cards, listen to the jazz, take the watches and the shoes of our acquaintances, engage in repartee appropriating everything we could from what we dimly understood to be a demi-monde of jazzmen and hipsters.

Actapublicorist entered dictionaries. Tokodynamometer and Turbofan.

When I got my hand inside her pants she said You know I never did let anybody do that and I'm pretty sure you shouldn't be the first. She stares out of her photograph. Going on eighteen and still a virgin just like all the rest of us and everyone we knew.

III

In four hours three minutes fifty two point two seconds Anatoly Vedykov walked for 50,000 meters. As for ourselves, we set no records. Neither at the gallop or the trot or the canter. Times got worse, we stayed out longer in the nights playing Scrounge or waiting for the final set at Marty's 502. I started calling 502 my distance. What's your distance? 440, right? In fact I've taken up the 502. After one jaunt around the oval feeling pretty good about my winnings on the night before I ran directly into Larson who had evidently clocked me. Christ, he said, you might as well have walked

the last four hundred yards with Anatoly Vedykov.

By 1960 you'd have heard
them all at Marty's: Monk and Miles, Coltrane,

Horace Silver, Sonny Rollins, even now and then
a white man like Giuffre.

                I liked Giuffre, the strange sound of his trio. I thought of it as 50,000 meters worth of walking music for the likes of Anatoly Vedykov. Larson used to play the records in the locker room incanting 440 502, 440 502. It must have seemed occult to anyone but us.

Trav'lin Light: studies in the application of La Violette's idea of slow-motion counterpoint. And then as JG said: because we're trav'lin round the country in a light Volkswagen bus and very light ourselves (minus bass and drums, & minus keyboard).

Giuffre alternating clarinet & tenor sax
Brookmeyer's valve trombone
Jim Hall: guitar

Pickin' 'em up and layin' 'em down.

In slow-motion counterpoint: Charles Van Doren
answers questions on TV inside a concentration booth:

Khrushchev bangs his shoe in the UN: Five to four
the Court upholds the power of Congress

to investigate subversives: Ingemar Johansson
knocks out Floyd Patterson: Joel Montgomery

spells correctly *fanfaronade*: Vanguard II is launched
to orbit for 100 years: Bobby Fisher turns 16.

       The quiz show scandal was a revelation to the
gullible: Van Doren, like the others, given answers in advance.
Who'd fight the Swede? who'd take off a shoe with old Nikita?
Bobby Fisher's rook-and-queen against a dragon variation of
Sicilian would spell fanfaronade in any bee. Or Fanfandango.
Farondole.

Had we not discovered Scrounge we might have found a game of
fan-tan at the Olentangy Village Chinese restaurant: beans, coins, &
counters in some hidden place. By 1961 Anatoly Vedykov would
still be walking. Explorer VI: fallen from the sky.

IV

Between your visits to the nursing home you burrow into all the
secret delves of what was once your house, turning up most
anything: decomposing diaries; a list of cities where you thought
you'd like to live; names for the year that has locked you in its book

on the Serengeti plain of Tanganyika or the streets of new
          Havana or the Himalayas
in Nepal. Year of the Missing Link year

of Fidel & Che year
of Edmund Hillary, of Anatoly Vedykov.

San Francisco Paris Rome or Venice Leningrad Palermo in Granada
Prague Vienna Perpignan Southend-on-Sea Tangier

                              or anywhere but here.

All your letters from the time you first left home and went to
          summer camp.
A thousand cancelled checks.
Poor Aunt Peggy's glasses labelled with a tie-on tag.

When Leaky found his skull our anthropology consisted of exam-
ining the heads we knew already frozen in the permafrost of
photographs and checking the cephalic index: broad or long, no
one looked entirely human. Had the photographer asked everyone
to smile and say *Zinjanthropus* he couldn't have done better: a class
of 1959 emerging one by one from some preconscious primate's
shadow just in time for a production of *The King and I* whose star
Yul Brynner clone would take up mortuary science.

Smile and say Zinjanthropus.
See you in Tangier.

Or in Santiago in the eastern Oriente provence or in Santa Clara in Las Vilas. First the local victories. Then an armored column moving on Havana. In the thinnest air, Edmund Hillary's on Mt. Makulu in Nepal. At 20,000 feet there's no sign of Yeti. You sign your name and sign your name again. The checks, the powers of attorney, living wills. You find the bottom lines and cross your t's.

Take me home she said don't sell the house I can't remember quite which one you are you know I really don't live here I'm only visiting.

Batista's visiting Dominican Republic. The Dalai Lama's visiting Bombay.

At 20,000 feet you can scarcely breathe at all.

We shaved his head in turns and eventually he was completely bald. He'd sing and dance. He'd wear the costume Mrs. Orr designed herself to much applause. In twenty years he'd get his thin embalmer's hands on Mrs Orr and Miss Kirkpatrick, on Mrs. Jones and Mr. Michelson and Mr. Todd. He'd stand discretely at the edge of things while those of us who still were left in town would pay our last respects. He'd give your mother your Aunt Peggy's glasses labelled with a tie-on tag.

He'd hang Costello's derby on the hatrack in the hall.

V

Old hat millineries made their mark:
the derby was a hit. Also slouch, fedora, swagger,

even Cossack. Down at the heel you'd find a dangerous spike,
you'd see a leopard stole, then an otter trench,

maybe even Jules François Crahay the man himself.
Hobble skirt. And after Fashion, Finland.

K.A. Fagersholm had fallen. R. Buckminster Fuller next.
Geodesic domes for radar on the DEW Line.

Distant Early Warning scanned the millenary sky.

When teleologists took Alpha from our almanac, Omega wept.
Rebel hit-men on the margin became hatters. Barkan, Binkley,
Bowen, Cash; Giles, Goss and Griffin. What were they to
Advertising, Aeronautics? Taken from aback, Zoetrope and Zero;
but underneath the photographs such confidence: Not a single
future written off as bankrupt. Nor as death from aneurysm. Not
a battered bride. These who'd be the doctor lawyer businessmen
and engineers demand a potency beyond their prime and poten-
tate. Look at Shah Mohammed smiling warmly from his page. Why
ever should he not? He married young Queen Farah in December
and is hoping for a male heir

as Lunik III observes the far side of the moon and Don Fidel the
progress of a hundred executions in a single hot and humid after-
noon.

Throw, the saying goes, your hat into the ring

                                      but first you put
your tennis shoes into the pot. Only then to leave, broke and bare-
foot, your corner table at the 502 for Cora's house at twelve, head

all full of Bird and Monk and Miles. She'd be waiting there all right, standing at the doorway in her shorts and bathed entirely in yellow light. You felt like Edmund Hillary at 20,000 feet.

Or like Costello's derby hanging in the hall.

A darker horse than Sister Life had never won a race. If David Lean could feast a few years later on Zhivago and convince Omar Sharif he was a poet, I could dance my Sister to the Millenary Ball and call her Cor (a.k.a. Omega Alpha). There we'd make the milliners all eat their hats. Dave Goss ate his hat. And Stephen Husted ate one. Harry Cash consumed a blue beret. Ruth McCallister nibbled at a pill box daintily. Randy Miller and his friend Sam Woodruff both ate busbies while our future General Patton, off to West Point in the fall, broke a tooth off on his helmet.

You thought, of course, the future would be yours—as did Che and JFK. Instead you'd be the future's, which would make a meal of you. One and one by one to cower in its flame as works and days unnumber and you do forget well almost all of it the whole damn thing gone blank in time and you too on the list with Raymond Chandler Errol Flynn and Amy's mother Florence Smith. Blue wave.

Tokodynamometer, my love, and Turbofan. Amen. Far out on the plain of Tanganyika. A pair of glasses labelled with a tie-on tag. A scattering of Pesos, Drachmas, Yen.

Part Two

I

America First or Lend-Lease. 1941.
The Christmas holidays at last and New Year's Eve.

How to measure now and
then and now again and in the mind

or then as now for all of them in kin & kind.
And how conceive.

How to parse out features in a body of the past
that took its measures . . .

Among the old prescriptions, bottles, and bandaids, *Married Love* (of
1936) moulders in a cabinet. Illustrated in a modest way for the
fastidious, it's clear enough: and you yourself the end of all instruc-
tion and a digit added to the census come September. They'd listen
to a fireside chat like everybody else. They'd sit beside their radio
and smoke their Lucky Strikes. No Third Term they'd chanted with
their friends. They're quiet now

listening to a man before the network microphones adjusting his
pince-nez. He speaks the words Great Arsenal. He tries out fear:
Spies already walk the streets of Washington. He says you cannot
reason with incendiary bombs, and looks into the eyes of Carole
Lombard sitting there with twenty others who have jammed into
the little room to hear this live. Your father stands, walks out to the
kitchen porch and looks up at the sky trying to imagine what it's
like in London. Your mother's thinking of that night they danced
to Jimmy Dorsey's band.

Or Paul Whiteman. Maybe Guy Lombardo, called by *Down Beat*
magazine the King of Corn. In the photograph you turn up in the
desk, they stand beside their old De Soto parked beside the north-
east corner of the house. First car. First house.

First war to be entirely theirs. The last was for the eldest

not the younger sons. For Edward, say, who sits alone in
    darkness

in a corner of the old Glen Echo house unvisited.
Doughboy with the Spanish flu, then encephalitis, he'd dance

to Guy Lombardo if he could but he can barely stand;
his walk's a kind of shuffle when he walks.

Named for his father who had ridden San Juan Hill
with Teddy R, the name came down on you

like some genetic ton of bricks: johnEdward. Edward.
Edward Edward Edward . . .

But then you're not a part of all this yet. It's only New Year's Eve.
Great Arsenal is still a phrase and not a thousand tanks, not a bill
before the house, not a wound to Charles Lindbergh, hero isola-
tionist, who'd flown so far it seemed so long ago.

II

They'd listen to Jack Benny once a week. Brought to you by Jell-O.
They'd go out to the films: Errol Flynn and Ronald Reagan chased
John Brown to Harpers Ferry; Abbott got so angry that he made
Costello cry. Rosebud someone told them was the codename for a
German agent, not what William Randolph Hearst had called his
mistress's

obscene that word if you can think of it Louella Parsons
Hedda Hopper said and recommended censorship

in time of war
a cenogenesis for every member cenobitical

eventually a cenotaph erected
in your own back yard with every name

you'd carve on every tall Glen Echo oak
in stone

Rosebud? Tricycle in fact.
Turned by MI5 to double on the Lisbon Abwehr, Dusko Popov
brought his microdot to Hoover at the FBI who didn't get the
import of the drawings questions diagrams regarding amunition
dumps the hangars installations on the warf the workshops dry
docks airfields naval operations in Hawaii. After Benny, newsman
Walter Winchell trashed the *glowering boy the sullen tot of history
the corn-fed Spengler stalking through the family dining room with
clouded brow a darkling child at our feast.* Your mother thought he
should be president; your father thought he should be shot. He
flew so far it seemed so long ago.

This year Scott Fitzgerald died and Henri Bergson Kaiser Wilhelm
Joyce Virginia Woolf and Robert Baden-Powell the founder of the
Boy Scouts. Sherwood Anderson Tagore and Robert Bridges also on
the list with Lou Gehrig and the voice of Earle Graser known to
every child as The Lone Ranger. It's hard to think of Graser's horse

without a rider someone on a soundstage horseshoes in his hands
who'd gallop them beneath the microphone on sand and sawdust
spread out in a box. Who'd say weep my love for

Nazi aces Mölders and Udet
the Prussian officer the SS Einsatzgruppen shot outside of
Leningrad. Tsvetayeva got through to Moscow then to Pasternak
at Peredelkino to Pasternak who didn't say you will be safe right
here my poet stay with me my love I'll call you Sister Life. She
hanged herself and three days later I was born.

That would be September. Now they measure bauxite for incendi-
aries chromium for armor plate copper for de-gaussing appara-
tuses to use against magnetic mines magnesium and manganese
for alloys

lead tin nickle zinc and tungsten.

They went out to the corner deli for dessert walking back along the
old Glen Echo drive where icy branches of the winter trees clicked
against each other silvering in moonlight. That night Edward died.
And RKO let Kane sit on the shelf three months even though the
word was out on Rosebud. Densko Popov said my name is Densko
Popov and I've come from Lisbon on my tricycle to help you break
their codes.

III

97-shiki O-bun In-ji-ki J-machine
a rat's baffle cry for cryptanalysis

a rising son whose father came from Kishinev
to sell them on how well the Singer sewed

sold them measurements of matrices
enciphering a system of successive

polyalphabetic substitutions and the wonder was
DiMaggio had fifty hits

in fifty games with everybody in the country counting and the
wonder was the Brits had cracked Enigma too at Bletchly Park as
Bertolt Brecht settled into Hollywood. Three years later I would ride
my yellow tricycle round and round the dining table while the old
Victrola played out *McNamara's Band*. When the music went all sour
I'd dismount and turn the crank until I couldn't turn it any more.
McNamara gave them twenty records when he learned about the
pregnancy and one of them was *McNamara's Band*.

Meet Marlene Dietrich, Peter Lorre, Thomas Mann, Stravinsky:
Yamamoto wearing his enciphered purple robes. Codename Fixer.
Codename Trickster. Fliegerhauptmann Lindbergh. Fliegerhaupt-
man Hess.

That year measured distance by unusual means. Home plate to left
field wall, degree of arc required to hook a fist in Billy Conn's
protesting open mouth, miles south from Flynn's estate to child
prostitute and Nazi agent in a single room, leagues required to get
your sea legs on the exile ship as sonar signals rippled out in waves.
Fliegerhauptman thought he saw the coast of Scotland, looped his
Messerschmitt, and parachuted down before the unbelieving eyes
of Piers the plowman standing there at dusk near Eaglesham
who'd take a measure more than Lindbergh's take a measure
rather less than Hess.

He caught the outside curve and drove it to the wall He bloodied
him at last and down he went like Schmeling smartass whiteboys
come on quiet nights to lose their innocence He put his hand
directly up her skirt and she did not say no don't do it didn't say
a thing and so He turned the crank until he couldn't turn it any
more and put on *McNamara's Band.*

He touched her rosebud it was manganese in alloy
it was allies it was axis
when she hanged herself and three days later you were born

like all these other codes and secret agents—
works of days apocalyptical foreseen by even Catalan Ramon
who spun configured mysteries on interlocking disks

to make an *ars inventiva veritatis* of the nine attributes of God.

Rat's baffle cry who'd haiku now DiMaggio my hero Errol Flynn my
Messerschmitt my Spirit of St. Louis and by Louis's right cross and
uppercut *Yo no naka wa jigoku no ue no hanami kana:* world's middle
       walking on the roof of hell
            and flower gazing!

IV

Kata kana over purple and in open code the short-wave-east-wind-rain. Yamamoto: Does it seem as if the birth is immanent? *Higashi No Kaze Ame.* It had been a healthy boy brought to term in all good time who'd twist the dials of his interlocking disks or ride a yellow tricycle around his room to wind up magic blow the east wind back uncloud the dark horizon that a hard rain down could never rain. He'd made an *ars inventiva veritatis* of the nine attributes of God

he'd walk the dog. Dog days. Dogtooth violets fringing sidewalks in his neighborhood. Long ago his Mendelian studies of the polypeptide chains. Who'd gazed on flowers walked the roof of hell and at his back heard echoes from Atlantic wolf packs answering their kin in kind: No kata kana haiku now or Yamamoto open code but lost sailors whispering *Jeder Engel ist schrecklich.*

Angels danced on conning towers, flight decks, the tips of wings. Fast tödliche Vögel.

McNamara had this problem with his inner ear. He said I think we'll just use Navahos or Cherokees the way the Brits have used Maltese. No one understands a wretched word of it. I'm so unsteady I can barely walk but still the beauty of it is I won't be draftable and neither I should think will you with that rheumatic heart. They slept through Bach at Disney's new *Fantasia.* They even slept through Rimsky-Korsakov and Chernobog Triumphant who would terrify you in due time and make you cry. Fast tödliche Engel. You'd hold your mother's hand.

These two buddies never went to war. They didn't have the heart for it, they didn't have the ear. They dug up McNamara's yard to plant tomatoes and zucchini where I'd help them pull up weeds in '45. They planted cantaloupe and carrots and potatoes. Their blushing melons and their apprehensive wives grew big all summer long decoding Mendel's laws. Mandrake Europe shrieked in Chernobog's right hand and Disney loosed the FBI on Hollywood. *The place was full of lousy Communists and they were worse*

than Nazis and the Japs. Even my friend Eisenstein who'd shaken hands
with Mickey went back home to Moscow fawning over Stalin like a daffy
duck.

Early August and die Vögel gazing down at Leningrad:
Walpurgis Nacht conducted by the Wehrmacht.

Sedarim read out Haggadah the 14th of Nisan
but every path of exodus was cut.

Every angel terrified. Every angle squared.
Every square enciphered as a circle.

You could sing like Chaliapin you could fight like Alexander
Nevsky but you might as well lie doggo and just pray for snow like
Sergei Mikhailovich in Alma Alta. Tapping on his telegraph in
Kinderspiele calling USA he'd whisper

Uncle Walt!

I look around me now and somehow think I see you in this fire
all your totems and your metamorphoses. Animism here's our way of life.

Every loaf of bread we bake can creep away.
Every stone along the narrow streets can mock us.

Every mouse that's left alive can weep.

V

One and one by one. The flower in the flame.
The manganese and armor plate and tungsten.

They went out to the corner deli walking back along
the old Glen Echo Drive and then she thought she felt the first
contractions. Someone on a soundstage with horseshoes in his
hands would gallop there beneath a microphone on sand and
sawdust spread out in a box. Horse without a rider. He'd said to her
one day you will be safe right here my poet stay with me my love I'll
call you Sister Life.

Hiding in the vast Pacific swells were *Zuikaku* and *Akagi* while the
old fusilier who would speak to you one day, shell shocked from
the other war and neurasthenic, stood not far from Dover among
failing numina of kin and kind looking for an efficacious sign.

Higashi No Kaze Ame. Jeder Engel ist schrecklich.

When teleologists put Alpha in their almanac, Omega danced.
Rebel hit-men on the margin got their hammers. Disney,
Lindbergh, Louis, Flynn; Benny, Abbott, Hopper. What were they
to Aachen, Aaron's rod? Taken from aback, Zipangu and Zion; and
underneath the photographs such confidence: Not a single future
written off to buzzbombs. Nor as death from Zyklon. Not a battered
bride. Those who'd be the doctor lawyer businessmen and unac-
knowledged legislators all demand a potency beyond their prime.
Look at young Johannes smiling from his page. Why ever should he
not? He married Miss Kirkpatrick last December and is hoping for
a male heir.

Take me home she said don't sell the house I can't remember quite
which one you are you know I really don't live here I'm only visit-
ing. God is subtle He is not malicious Einstein said and Eisenstein
of Chernobog He is a code.They show them movies in the nursing
home. I know when I was born but can't remember how it felt.

When they bought their blackout curtains down at Woolworth's
McNamara took his box of wooden nickels from a shelf and buried
it among the blackened frosted melons in his garden. You could
also blast your lithium with deutrons and irradiate your mercury
for gold. You could sign up with Enrico Fermi and get rich on U-
235.

You could dance with her to Guy Lombardo
look at all the photographs drive the old De Soto down the streets
of 1941
and knock out Billy Conn.
You could sell the yellow tricycle to Densko Popov sew a shroud on
Singer push the Lend-Lease bill in Congress measure bauxite for
incendiaries split the atom drop the bomb dismantle DNA and find
a proper setting for the cenotaph.
But that won't bring Lou Gehrig up to bat or put a Ranger in the
empty silver saddle.

Zeros were reported flying in the skies above L.A. Alphas and
Omegas over San Francisco. Take me home she said don't sell the
house I can't remember quite which one you are you know I really
don't live here I'm only visiting.

One and one by one remembers quite and who you were
Rerhüf, Retarf, Retam, Otomamay . . .
                         Visiting.
Alphas and Omegas on their way to Aachen.
Zipangu and Zion.
        Noiz Noiz.   U   gnp   z.

Part Three

I

Russian MIGs & Mau Maus. Dead Sea scrolls & Piltdown men.
You heard they'd executed Beria.
They'd execute the Rosenbergs, but not the ones you knew.

That girl in World History came down with Polio.
Or was it Civics? Or did she get TB?
In 1953 we got TV. Nearly everyone we knew already had it.

His joke the year before when we were still the last among our
friends to get it was to point me down the basement stairs and say
I got us one go have a look—at the Bendix, it turned out, spinning
water down its drain to end the cycle and my mother smiling there
about to hang my shirts and sheets and underclothes up on the
line. But politics had forced his hand eventually: he'd wanted Joe
McCarthy in his living room and so I got Lucille Ball and he got Roy
Cohn and all of us got *Dragnet* and the Coronation. I also got a
camera with a flash attachment that would make me popular with
Ned's precocious sister Nell.

You wanta kiss my sister?

           ————————?

           I'd take her picture
though. Let's do fashion shots, she'd often say. She must have been
fifteen. She must have shown you Ralph Marino silhouettes, Mollie
Parnis satin collars, Skinner crepes, Dior's Maxime with folded
cummerbund and cinching narrow waist with deep and strapless
décolletage. This, she'd say, is my bodice. And this is my breast.
You'd flash your bulb.

More fraudulent than your pornography the Piltdown find as
printed once again in glossy mags—that skull, that jaw. *Eoanthropus
dawsoni* took no oath with Adam Mumbi and Gikuyu but his spec-
tographic studies conjured Mau Mau out of Aramaic for the deute-
rocanonical echt deutsch.

Who'd cast Dorris Day as Ethel Rosenberg? Who'd present
to Eisenhower Beria's pince-nez?
Stern declension down this year as Jim Thorpe died

and Dylan Thomas Robert Taft Prokofiev Picabia
and Uncle Max of natural causes
more or less and only Julius & Ethel on the list electrocuted
      Beria just shot.

That year all nephology seemed neomorphic all neology unneigh-
borly: Communists might also be good citizens said Mrs. Lynch
who lost her job for telling us just that when she had finished read-
ing us aloud that Mayakovsky play *A Cloud in Pants.*

      And on the new TV such news: his list
of enemies identified in government his hand upraised his posse
a Poseidon of a force his posture so remote from hers who came
to us from London on that tiny screen and was anointed with the
oils from a gold ampulla with a tiny spoon. *Te Deum Laudamus* they
sang. Regalia were passed around and they arrayed her with
Colobium Sidonis and then handed her the spurs the orb the ring
the sceptre with the cross the rod and dove. Her photograph sped
round the world

      but Nell's I hid away. Sherpa Tensing near the
top of Everest, I took the south col dreaming of Nepal.

II

You'd play at mountaineering down in what the others called *the glen* but you called *the ravine* because your parents did. You'd also do the Bedouins exploring Dead Sea caves. You'd do Korean War and Mau Mau massacres. Along the Khumbu Glacier up the icefall hacking steps and fixing ropes, you'd pull up Ned who'd fall exhausted in your arms at over 20,000 feet. You'd make your camp and wait until the lovers came in cars.

It may be the Essenes invented Satan
but my father thought it was Supreme Court Liberals

like Douglas who'd reverse him and his colleagues on appeal.
He too was Supreme, but only in Ohio,

"sitting on the bench" like some poor third string guard.
He'd sup on his suppositories. Our cave had

turned up parchments wrapped like mummies in old earthen
     jars
& we found psalms, beatitudes, sundry sapiential works

and Messianic rules. Also a Masonic ring we traded to the Brits
for their binoculars.
           . . . . *ytlh 'nsym hyym, wtlytmh 'wtw*
'l h's wymt—He hangs the men alive! You shall hang him on the tree
and he shall die. For passing information to an enemy, e.g. For
delivering one's people up: *Epikataratos pas ho kremamenos epi xylou.*
And then we found the spoons and buttons, needles, nails, & coins.
We found a dildoe and a dilly bag. Between your visits to the nurs-
ing home the CIA declassifies Venona: now you know Antenna
Calibre and Goose were agents back in Babylon and Tyre.

         & in the drawers & closets of your mother's
house those spoons and buttons from the cave. Also baseball cards
and Marvel comic books, Qumran's pesharim, letters from
Antenna, photographs of Nellie as Maxime.

Among the word lists for a new vocabulary circa new half-century
you'd chainjack way downrange a firestorm's megadeath.
You'd back-breed in 3-D at burnout speed.

Ethel ran the deli down on Hudson Street beside the movie house
my mother called "the picture show." That's Ethel *Rosenberg*.
Neighbors asked her if she knew the other one the atom spy or if
she'd change her name or did she know Klaus Fuchs and all those
others in the news. She'd drop a bagel in your dilly bag without
so much as saying Old Los Alamos although she'd whisper in your
ear non sequitur's tautologies. Sunset over the ravine as Red
Chinese and North Koreans climbed up Pork Chop Hill.

We'd dug in deeply waiting for the air support. Focusing
        binoculars
on hands of unsuspecting lovers

who were groping at each other's crotch
sprawled out on the back seat of their Mercury convertible

I didn't see the sniper crouched above us
under outcrop stone until he fired.   The report

was filed away as classified; the mission order was *abort*.

III

Things your mother said from time to time
are all she ever says today forgetting mostly any speech at all
but Georgetown's by the river
picture show e.g. & don't stay out past eight in the ravine & don't
go to the swimming pool you'll get exposed to polio he'll take you
in the motorcar & shut the blinds and windas good night nurse
I'd just as leave I'd just as soon and you out yakin on the daven-
port asfarasezconcern that record on the gramaphone'll make me
nervous as a cat.

We'd go to triple features at the Hudson. *Bwana Devil, House of Wax,
The Charge at Feather River.* Objects hurled at us from the screen.
Sitting in the dark and wearing Polaroids we didn't think of objects
hurling through the sky but all the 52s up there were practicing
LeMay's attack on Leningrad by nuking down electric duds on
Dayton and Columbus. You go to Hillside House with Alzheimer's
and drool. Otherwise you get a window with a view and lots of
Xanax.

She tells you she's in Georgetown and at school
says it's spring it's autumn now she knows because her ears are red
she says it's nice outside and would you like some lemonade.

See they masturbate like we do with this clitoris right here.

Ned had recently acquired a Kinsey and was pointing at a diagram.
Nell would open up her labia and smile. As the congregation sang
out *I was glad* the scholars of Westminster exercised their right
acclaimed their sovereign shouting *vivat vivat* as she made her way
along the choir. She put her golden girdle on & tried the spurs on
the Archbishop who presented her the Rod as massed trumpets
sounded & as cannon at the Tower fired salutes.

Could you back-breed objects like a race horse hurl a chainjack into
Oppenheimer's calculations? Bohr and Heisenberg were only made
of observations on the day we took down all the orbiting electrons

from the model and Professor Einstein poured out drinks for Dylan
Thomas on a field of praise he'd failed to unify.

That's why Dark Star nosed out Native Dancer in the Derby.

That's why teleology had hidden *De Re Militari* in a cave
and Ethel Rosenberg smiled like Mona Lisa

and the Pumpkin Papers that convicted Alger Hiss
convinced the archaeologists at Khirbet Qumran.

Piltdown jaws away at time gone tipsy as we scar our faces rubbing
red clay in our wounds and take our oaths. Beria broke down
completely wept and begged them for his life. He'd give them
dachas by the sea, he'd give them Stalin's pets and playmates,
Lenin's secret penthouse in New York. They dragged him down the
corridor and down the stairs and pushed him to his knees against
the wall. They shot him with a pistol in the brain.

That's why both her ears are red it's nice outside and would you
like some lemonade.

That's why by the outcrop stone one summer night when no
        moon rose up over the ravine
and I was watching *I Love Lucy* or *The Red Skelton Show*
Ned committed incest with his sister
                            or it wasn't why.

IV

He only said he did it and he really didn't.
He didn't really do it but he bet she said he did.
She said he did it but she didn't know he couldn't when he
        didn't do it and she said.
He said I really did it but she didn't know it.

Then Kikuyu Central spoke up for Kenyatta. We all prayed solemnly
to missionary god Mwathani Ngai but to old Mwene old Nyaga too.
We ate the meat of Miss Kirkpatrick's dachshund and of Mr.
Macintosh's cat, pierced the sodom apple & the sheep's eye with
our thorns. They passed a calabash of blood around our shaven
heads and we traded them our foreskins for their cigarettes.

As members of the forest gang we'd hamstring livestock, burn the
grain stores, terrify the Europeans with machetes. Then we heard
about the Vietminh and thought we'd drive the French into the
sea. Even so the *Isle de France* had its attractions and we saved a crew
of twenty-six whose freighter sank in mid-Atlantic storms.

No one said you were the Mortgenröthemensch, but I ask you was
that jaw Orangutang? That year patination of a Van Dyck brown
was revealed as potassium-bichromate stain. You wore your pilt-
down cranium like Uncle Edward's blue beret and found the hippo
bones out in the quarry.

Disasters follow dermatology precede
disciples and discrimination in employment. First up in the Es is
Eastern Orthodoxy but you'd never met the Patriarch in Istanbul
and neither he would lay you odds
had Julian schismatics like Chrysostom Cavouridis.

Epikataratos pas ho kremamenos epi xylou.

She walked along the golden carpet toward the royal gallery and
Chair of the Estate. Judges, bishops, officers and peers were in their
stalls. They offered her the bread. They offered her the wine. The

congregation sang *All People That On Earth Do Dwell*. Then they placed the leather strap across her mouth and dropped the hood and buckled down her arms and wrists and legs. When the current hit her body it appeared as if she tried to stand, her hands shrivelled into furious little fists.

In the Abbey everybody cheered. Your mother said your father's right you give them back their cigarettes and don't stay out past eight in the ravine. Take me home she said don't sell the house I can't remember quite which one you are you know I really don't live here I'm only visiting.

And eschatology took Ethel from our alphabet and made Good
        Friday dance
listening to Crusoe on the juke box and with Julius already gone.

He'd pierce the sodom apple & the sheep's eye with his thorn.
He'd hamstring livestock join the Vietminh or meet schismatics
        for a lemonade.
He'd telephone Kikuyu Central for the Mortgenröthemensch.

We did the executions readily enough, strapping one another down and playing anthems on an old kazoo. Nell prefered to play the queen but she was also good at making little fists & jerking from the hips when hit by say two thousand volts delivered at a full eight amperes.

He said she did it but he didn't know she couldn't when she didn't do it and he said.

V

A little Ritalin a little Prozac or a Zoloft if you please. These
Mothers for a Mild Millennium; these Ladies for a Later Lexicon.
Telekenetic, though, and Sabbaterian. She says it's like the
hoosegow here you know the callaboose the clink the lockup
where they send the sinners overdosed on neuroleptics and you'd
better come another day.

Beneath the overhang of weeping-willow limbs
propped in wheelchairs beside the quiet waters and decidedly
          another day—
their voices made of lilac
and their gestures made of hay.

In the summer Ned and Nell were saved. They'd shout and sing. At
the Pentecostal Church you'd pass that looked like some aban-
doned warehouse with a whitewashed cross nailed to a plain black
door. She gave up fashion shows and executions and we all gave
up the Mau Mau massacres and Khumbu Glacier climbs. They'd
met the Mortgenröthemensch and it was them. While I stood
listening by a window terrified to go inside they'd sing their cipher
out like KGB cryptologists before their time. They'd speak in
languages the slain in spirit know their xenogloss an antiphon to
all the glossolalias of man.

That September I returned to school. Everyone seemed all at once
to be thirteen. We'd crouch beneath long tables in the cafeteria,
hook our arms behind our heads protecting face and neck against
the flash. It was a drill. It was the bomb. Somehow we'd survive if
we could just protect that tender flesh that burned.

You wondered crouching there how many had been saved. Was
          Eisenhower saved?
Was Syngman Rhee? You hunkered down.

How about Kenyatta and Chrysostom Cavouridis?

The men up there in 52s the men in MIGs the men in missile
        silos in Ukraine?

Were Ethel at the deli and the Ethel in the Chair and
        executioner Francel and the Essenes?
Tell me Joel about the former rain about the latter rain the later
        lexicon the prophecy and weeping willows by the quiet
        waters and the lemonade.

And underneath a table in a cave or overhang of weeping willow
limbs or down a glen or in an abbey or an execution chamber
someone says you did it when you didn't or you really didn't when
you really did and hands you the binoculars a gold ampulla with
a little spoon a ticket to *The House of Wax* an orb a sodom apple and
a thorn. Forget the foreskins and the cigarettes. And no need for
the spectographic studies if you're targeted because you'll only be
a shadow on the ruins of a cafeteria wall.

Dawnman was a mensch all right and in this country anything is
possible O dim and lonely Piltdown bluff it's great it's Greek to me.

So what's to say at Pentecost if no one wears a satin collar spreads
her labia and takes a picture or a Zoloft or an oath or all the orbit-
ing electrons from the model stays out late in the ravine and nails
a porkchop to the flagpole in the middle of the camp.

Gloss it from the glossolalia as *epi xylou: qillat ĕlōhîm tālûy.*
Chainjack way down range
a firestorm's megadeath and back-breed in 3-D.

A shirt blown off of somone's back is hanging like a banner in a
        blasted tree.

Part Four

I

The year before I'd worked for ninety cents an hour shuffling IBM
cards people folded spindled mutilated I suppose it looked as
though I sat there playing solitaire I had to earn enough to get
somehow to what I called Constantinople what I called Byzantium
in spite of all for she had gone to Turkey with her family Cora had.
Her file was her father's double A for Architecture Archeology okay.

One long year alone and counting
her anatomy in drifting mind in reverie at work while auditing
those spindlefolded mutilates her architecture

she had offered me when we were seventeen
had placed my hand deliberately on her ass as we stood blinking
at the sidelines in the autumn mist & watched

our classmates gallop on some county football field

never even had you been away from home more than a month or
so in Michigan perhaps Wisconsin just some family holiday and
now you muttered to yourself beginning yet another box of Aakers
Aarons and Abairs about the gold mosaics on a wall about the
hammered gold and gold enameling and brought up sharply by
Abdallah Joseph Abdel-Rahman Zenebee.

1961 this time. Box and volume index income tax and yearly
rebate post or posting or to claim oh Abbett Brenda Abel Betty
Abernathy Charles.
Ave or avaunt there Axelrod and Aycock Ayres Ayu Azzarito LJ
Babbit a new beat.

His letters home from 1926 this time are somehow boxed with
mine from Istanbul he's at the Belview Biltmore Florida and always
writes in pencil always says Dear Folks he's someone in these
letters that I never knew he's happy having beaten the rheumatic
fever having just got up and on his feet I guess he hasn't met my
mother yet he's only twenty-one and didn't have to think about

the neurofibrillary tangles in his brain the helicals in pairs the
microtubules or
tau proteins phosphorylated beta-amyloids
or chromosome fourteen.

Russians that year orbited the earth. That put everybody on alert in
Anatolia including Cor. You gambled all your Betas and abandoned
Amy Loid at the Helical way out in Tau betting no one found the
gene for chromosome fourteen and paid your way by IBM by audit
and by alphabet. And Ernest Hemingway blew out his brains in
Idaho.

Between the shuffles of an Axelrod
Telli Babba blessed a virgin on the Bosphorus and physics

blasted nuclei to mason rho and meson pi.
Biochemistry induced the birth of a synthetic RNA.

You wondered if the Hittites took cuneiform from the Assyrians if
Phocaeans emigrated west if Pax Romana could dissolve in olive oil
and wine and could you get there on the Gnostic airlines before
June if Constantine intended first of all to rebuild Troy.

II

All so long ago it seems hallucinated now. Eighteen. And walking
by the Black Sea with your suicidal love. Your letters home a
tourist's recitation or resuscitation not to be resisted in recitative.
Her body your obsession and your pockets full of condoms spilling
in their silver wrappers in the sand.
Rhapsodists rewired then with rhenium for rhyme.
It wasn't Florida in 1926 dear folks.

Elsewhere it is always midnight always Maidenek and Belsen.
Transportation officers subordinate he says Servatius arguing
against the jurisdiction of the court. The man himself behind his
glass and taking notes in pencil on a little pad. A tool in the hands
of a malignant fate he says. Abducted from the Argentine.
Malignant fate a tool. His hands malignant as his fate. His tool in
his hands.

Hotel. Oh tell O'Tool.
In what far lands against what falling evil. And in what mirror in
what twisting corridor you'd find this Amy Loid this chromosome
fourteen and not remember any more.
You'd wear a Fez you'd finger strings of little beads you could

right now drive past her house by making just a tiny detour on the
way back to the nursing home. The architect her father's still alive.
She herself you haven't seen for almost thirty years. And would you
recognize her now. And would she know the graybeard sitting in
his car and staring stupidly at her front door. Everything as strange
just down the road as down the years. Hotel. Oh tell. Her legs
spread open there but ah her lips astounding you with I must tell
you that while you've been gazing moonily upon my yearbook
picture for three thousand years I've had so many men you could-
n't count them all.

You'd count them all. There's Ajax Agamemnon and Achilles and
there's Atatürk and General Yassiada Nazim Hikmet Yuri A Gagarin
Sultan Abdul Hamid and his seven sons John Foster Dulles and

Makarios of Cyprus all of them successful down the road or down
the years although it must be said that Gary Cooper
Ty Cobb Dashiell Hammett
Carl Gustav Jung Dag Hammarskjöld Sam Rayburn Eero
        Saarinen
and Ernest Hemingway (already mentioned) died.

Onomastics no has nothing in the world to do
with Onan son of Judah or the onager a stone-propelling engine
of the siege the wild ass of central Asia no it's just

a listing of the folks a kind of wedding invitation
or a seating plan the order of an execution
it's a catalogue of ships. I'm really loving this amazing summer

here upon the plains of Anatolia near the winedark sea.
So what if she has had this little thing with Abdul Hamid
and the boys oh and yes the other little things

(fill in at will the names provided on your list).
It's me she really loves. The postcard shows
you Hisarlik where Heinrich Schliemann dug up Troy.

That's me beside the gallows where they hung Menderes in July.
The transportation officer is on the right.

III

Displacement of the *c* and *h* invests the *gens* and so it's
Eigen isn't Eich or Manicore if vertebrate is shown

he may inherit in his haunted house regressive genes
more readily if organisms crave their transportation

into cave the better to survive in Konya you could ruminate
on Rumi like a troglodite

rummy or canasta was
the game she played the game you see them playing still up on the
second floor in wheel chairs their minds still there still focussed on
the playing cards whose own dear folks had not transported chro-
mosome fourteen.

Dear Folks: We took the ferry from the European to the Asian side
in only twenty minutes; then we sailed down the coast. They
brought us tea in little glasses as the sky line full of minarets began
to fade. Effendi stood up by the rail shouting *spaka gimek*. Literally
that means put on a hat. Shoes on feet and pants on legs a shirt
and tie a jacket and a waistcoat that's what old Mustafa Kemel said
he said whereas

in rummy or canasta you must meld. It's not the same in Rumi.
Sequence has no value suits no meaning here. You hope for jokers
and red threes. It's runic as can be among these Anglo-Saxons of
the second floor but would you play it on your melophone and
could you find a mandate in Koranic law?

He says at the conclusion—he is twenty-one, it's 1926—that he
would rather not come home would rather not go on to law school
disappointing news he understands but that is how he feels. He
hopes he says in some mysterious way to make his family proud
of him he says he hasn't taken any medicine at all these past three
months he feels confident he says he's happy now and he was I
would say a miserable man for his entire life he came back home

he studied law he married Lois K out there where she inherits in
her haunted house I visit her again I write it down.

That year retranslated Paul to the Ephesians retranslated John
while summer gaucho Klement alias the abductee the man expert
in sealed trains listened with his earphones looking darkly
through his glass. They'd take you to the Aesculapium where it was
written only death forbidden here and down into the tunnels
down into the basement temple where a priest of Pergamum
would whisper through the speaking tube be well be well

they drugged the hopeless cases absolutely dotty everybody
thought they heard the voice of a god

or at Nicaea or in 325.
Constantine held every joker every last red three.
Spaka gimek. Go put on a hat

in that hotel. Or walking by the winedark sea.
And swimming out in it—

Swimming out so far I thought she'd drown
I thought the only thing she wanted

was to die.

IV

Her father's job was reassembling temples. Expert also in the
Esperanto of assorted eschatologists and an impediment to your
desires he answered when the pedocals of arid regions called and
was a pedagogue whose pebbles were on offer to Pelagians. We
helped him dig and sift and sort.

It would have been a pagan holiday
all Roman baths and pornographic movies at the theatre

except for Paul & John & the apocalyptic angel
seven stars in his right hand & walking in the midst of all the
        archaeologists

the dervish dancing where sweet Artemis once dwelled
a reed plucked from her marsh a flute

bewailing separation from her bed of reeds

while at the nursing home they opened up the seventh seal. Then
she turned and in the moonlight by the temple gate undid her
bodice looking at you frankly and you saw at once the heaving of
her twenty breasts pearled in the tiny drops of a lactescent dew.
But if you harbor chromosome fourteen the time will come when
you remember none of this. Take me home she says don't sell the
house I don't remember quite which one you are you know I don't
live here I'm only visiting.

Canasta decks cascading to the floor. The sound of distant
castanets.

Dear folks: we disembarked at Port Coressus then passed through
the Harbor Gate and walked the length of marble pavement lined
with colonnades and shops until we reached the tetraphylon like
the one you know in Palestine. Once they isolated lepers as you will
recall but now it is the old like you who must be swept from the
agora off beyond the gate of Mithradates where we shut them up in

colonies as if old age itself were a contagion and they shuffle down
the hallways on their walkers sometimes lashing out with canes.
One old geezer Erosthostenes has said he knows a way to enter
history

to claim immortal fame he'll burn Diana's temple
down where after Ephesus the Es on offer
will include the epicycle and the epidemic and the epilogue

epiphany a feast on January 6 and Erebus a state of mind
resistant to epistemology the epsilon
equivocal but there on your escutcheon anyway

and so that's me again beside Effendi in my Fez. Heinrich
Schliemann on my left and on my right the hangman and the
judge. In Washington Casals is playing Allemandes for JFK in Upper
Arlington the ladies on the second floor are playing cards. My
father is in Florida it's 1926. No one drowns herself in that year's
southern sea. Effendi tells me go put on a hat. I said in what hotel.
I said not Onan son of Judah nor the onager.

Everybody on alert all over Anatolia.
Hotel. Or tell which temple eschatology rebuilds.

Which are you the epidemic or the epilogue. Oh epsilon my son!
45326 acknowledges his number in his glass.

V

Your story then. That too in the box. You called her Margaret there
and you yourself were Richard but not here. Your Istanbul looks
more like Alexandria than Istanbul. Doubtless you were reading
Lawrence Durrell who was hot in 1961. When the crazy family and
the randy lover of the eldest daughter get out to the ruins every-
thing implodes. But Margaret doesn't try to drown herself in any
sea. Hotel. I tell her father you can call me epsilon. He says I'll call
you Otto Ottoman I'll call you Byzantine Bill. I say they say your
daughter's fucking Abdul Hamid and his seven sons. He says we
disembarked at Port Coressus then passed through the Harbor
Gate and walked the length of marble pavement lined with colon-
nades and shops until we reached the tetraphylon like the one you
know in Palestine. He says they'd take you to the Aesculapium
where it was written only death forbidden here and down into the
tunnels down into the basement temple where a priest of
Pergamum would whisper through the speaking tube be well be
well

beware dear folks of eschatology he says the millineries
and their hats the radar
gazing at a millenary sky. She says Hotel. I know it's a hotel. I tell
     them
that I don't live here I tell them how

the rummy players meld
and how the transportation officer explains The Way. Tau
     proteins
form a halo around senile plaques.
He hopes to make his family proud of him he hasn't taken any
     medicine at all.

That was Cora and not Margaret swimming out to sea.

Your story then. A shuffle only in the IBMs detaches all the Aakers
from the Abdel-Rahman Zenebees. A shuffle only when you try to
walk. Hotel. A temple bell. A reed plucked from her marsh a flute

bewailing separation from her bed of reeds. You took the ferry from the European to the Asian side and then sailed down the coast. They brought in tea in little glasses as the sky line full of minarets began to fade. Effendi stood up by the rail shouting *spaka gimek*. Also Ephesus. Also SOS. And when she turned there by the temple she undid her bodice looking at you frankly and you saw at once the heaving of her twenty breasts. In that hotel. Her legs spread open there her lips astounding you with such bad news. You wondered if the Hittites took cuneiform from the Assyrians. You'd wear a fez. You'd finger strings of little beads although they didn't do it this way in Ohio.

At Catal Hüyük some 4000 years before Egyptian pyramids Diana's chthonic shape appears in figurines uncovered in the neolithic hills. Not far from Hisarlik. Not far from Upper Arlington where you drove slowly past her house those nights of playing Scrounge with Joel and Carl. She'd be there, all right, standing in her shorts and bathed entirely in yellow light. Your story then. You won't be overlooked by the geneticist.

You empty out the boxes one and one by one
your letters and your father's and your fictions

where you cower in the future's flame
as works and days unnumber and you do forget

well almost all of it the whole damn thing
gone blank in time and you too in the cards

with Zoetrope and Zero and the Zenebees.

Part Five

I

I think I heard him saying *and he still drinks alcohol*
and laughing like he'd said I still drank Kool Aid.
He himself of course "took drugs."
Three of us were pissing on a walnut tree.

That was I suppose at Jim Black's place up in Los Altos hills the year
when Al Guerard had tried to woo back west a scowling Irving
Howe by taking him to what he'd hoped would be sufficiently
outrageous student parties. <u>Dissent's</u> *Gone Soft On The Imperialists*
proclaimed a banner hanging up above the band. But on the other
hand.

Urinalysis of schizophrenics shows a trace of something like
Methoxyphenylethylamine.
Bump off every single nitrogen and your compounding chemist
grinds you up the flowering tops of those deflowered female
    hemps:
Tetrahydrocannabinol.

Polysyllables for Sixty-Six and you yourself polygamous almost.
Polyphonic anyway and polytheistic. Powers of attorney put you
in another's hands: & to perform which act and acts what thing
and things whatever the device and the devices in the law what-
ever may be needful necessary in my name to do to execute and to
perform it largely amply and to all intents and purposes as I might
do if I were present and performing it myself
shall never be
affected by my disability my incapacity
incompetence or lapse of time.

Two of us had lapsed into a corner of the time where coffee was the
thing at two a.m. We show each other poems. One of us is to
become the Poet Laureate. Not me. Poet Laureate of the United
States. Your sickly father was alive and came out to your wedding.
Your mother was quite fit and had no need to give up any power.
Your friend would marry you okay but did not love you welladay.

This was 1966. This was swimming in the Yangtze and a US H-
bomb missing in the sea near Palomares. This was the Miranda
case and anybody's right to stand up silently. This was mining
harbors in Haiphong apartheid in South Africa and Lin Piao on
culture. This was avalanche in Rio and a BOAC jet exploding at the
foot of Fuji. Claiming your Miranda rights
you'd stand up silently when asked
does anybody know a reason why this woman and this man

should not abide in Methoxyphenylethylamine
as long as they both shall live?

Your father would not now live long.
What's left of him I've packed up in a box with all his yearbooks.

All the books of all those years I've numbered here
to parse out features in a body of the past that took its measures

all dissent gone soft on the Imperialists
laughing like you drank some Kool Aid

lapsed into the corner of a time.

II

Most of magic in the drug you hoped they took was in the pill they
called the pill the period coming on like clockwork every month
and no more need for condoms or to come in someone's open
hands I loved it in the shower when she'd bend down with her wet
hair on my thighs and with her mouth almost although the one
you marry on inspired impulse may decide within a year you will
not do you kept it up with two or three you knew before her time
you'd grieve when she went off with R who knew more than the
rest of us about the war who'd been in combat in Korea no one
could believe he was that old.

God the druggist staring at me when I started in with Cora and
would have to ask for Trojan-enz with maybe who could tell some
colleague of my father's in the line behind me or the cousin older
sister aunt of someone in my class
and then you'd have to specify the lubricated kind and he'd
pretend he hadn't heard
and you at fifty-five remember this and impotent sometimes.

Beta blockers digitalis and its glycosides diazepam and half the
stuff you're on impair erections

even diuretics and the TAD's. And then he asked me if I still
        drank alcohol.
Mao and Lin Piao could tell you power was the real

aphrodisiac. But how much should you take and how long
should you take it and do benefits outweigh the risks?

Do I need to take any special precautions? Are there side effects
I should expect?

She tries to phone the street address and then sends off a letter to
the telephone: Martha Jane and Mary Kay at Hudson 43402. She
cannot understand the nurse who cannot understand her patient

when she says go get that man who fixes Gramaphones. I put the
yearbooks in a cardboard box. I do it largely amply and to all
intents and purposes as she might do it were she present and
performing this herself

in San Francisco by the Longshoreman's Hall.
And just like any tourist in the Day-Glo silent night whose Dada
        metamorphosis
could suffer an arrest and call it love.

That year Maoists starved their neurons and deprived their
neurofilaments of dopamine. Then they ran
like Mau Maus through Peking. Power was the proposition

power was the drug. And as I write that down
I hear a boom-box in the street I hear a voice that's disembodied
keening elegy for Captain Trips.

In San Francisco by the Longshoremen's Hall not a single cadre
dressed like peasants no one dragged the mayor from his bed or
burned his books or smashed his tablets in the public square. You
starved your neurons and deprived your neurofilaments of
dopamine by other means. Why not be a literalist of the imagina-
tion why not say the people's opium is opium. You did. Your dead.
You dithered there. Bore fraternal greetings to the Chief of State
to Liu Shao-chi to party General Secretary Teng Hsiao-ping and
begged them not to follow in the line that wound up from the
Wharf and to the cinema where everybody waited for Zhivago in
the dark and listened for the balalaika like a broken like a balabal-
abalalaika.

III

R had "occupied" the office of the president with several friends
from SDS. Now he's occupied as president himself. They sat around
the office drinking beer. We ourselves by then "took drugs." Three
of them were pissing on the walnut desk, dissent gone soft on the
Imperialists. Feet up on the gleaming surface, cigarettes stubbed
out in presidential tray, R concerned himself with dials that would
amplify the Dylan songs on out the window and across the quad.
And in an early poem the Laureate's red eye flashed from Palo Alto
"clean as malice" through the fog in Redwood City where they
made the napalm by the bay. He thought, he said, about the village
of Bien Hoa

so did you a little bit
and went to live in London out in Islington.

The nurse was fired who took her Demoral.
The Beatles were more popular than Jesus.

I suppose it's possible Akhmatova had died
the very moment Yuri first saw Lara as that movie

ran in London Paris San Francisco
& the paper opened up in someone's hands

        across the isle you were in the train the Circle
line you watched the movie thinking back on Sister Life you had
not been as you had thought you'd be the future's guest in some-
one's Poem Without a Hero but you overhear the nurse who
jabbers on just like your students saying *so I'm like and then he goes*

what was she like where did he go
that year that swallowed up Akhmatova Jean Arp André Breton
Montgomery Clift & Buster Keaton Hedda Hopper Admiral Chester
Nimitz Giacometti Frank O'Connor Disney. Married just six
months and now the ocean for a fact between us R had shown me
that book *Ariel* and asked me *Do you have a rubber crotch?*

97,000 there in Wembley and when Geoffrey Hurst kicks in the winning goal the country goes completely nuts even Harold Wilson and the Queen. 400,000,000 watch this on TV. The World Cup's elixir or a hemlock Dear you look so tired today. Franglais entered dictionaries. Aleotoric big bang theory camp.

REM and screen pass po-faced mini eldercare.
The Frug. The Hype.
Go-go jump-cut bonkers. Royal Shakespeare does the persecution of Marat performed by inmates of the Charenton asylum as directed by De Sade and Dr. Freidenberg. Mentation better once she went off Haldol and the Prozac back in February still she's in decline Language is aphasic Manifests agnosia and paranoia lately Gait is shaky and she'll need a cane. You'll notice frequently the verbal paraphasias. Word substitutions. DAT.

He reads the REMs hooks up electrodes
and determines which dementias can be classified AT.
Why not first unzip the rubber crotch.
Is that an evil eye my love or something newly alloy a prosthetic
        made of plastics
or a part that resurrects.

How does Komsomol serve Communism. Translate and provide
        your gloss.

IV

There you sat where Karl Marx once sat and wrote your London poems. All about divorce. You might have known you'd only manage such a theme even having come so far for revolution. Sit there long enough and maybe echoes from the roundhouse walls would penetrate. You couldn't concentrate. You smoked and drank. Fifteen minutes in the reading room and then an hour's break across the street with Players and a pint. Echoes from the round-house walls as you continue down the halls with plastic garbage bags.

A certificate that he attained the 33rd degree. Supreme court robe. Campaign buttons all the way from Harrison and Grant. A drawer entirely full of corks. Another full of soy sauce containers. Plastic compact in a bathroom cabinet there among the decades old prescriptions and you lift it open with a finger nail in surprise behold

her diaphragm. Diabolic how they'll give you diacetylmorphine for just a simple case of diachronics. Diagnosis at some weird diagonal to diakinesis. You sat there at your desk to diagram the dialectic but regretted you had never danced the old diaspora before Diaghilev completed his dialysis.

Nurses wheel their patients in and run the film. On a screen the size of Mt. Olympus geriatric porn queens lick each other's cunts. An imagery the Laureate declared in his first book consisting like America in lack of scale. Back there in the distance is Zhivago trudging through the snow. He's on the scent. Up ahead are Lara Beatrice Penelope and Cor. Mao had virgins brought in by the dozen, never took a bath, wouldn't brush his teeth. For months on end did not get out of bed. Take me home she said don't sell the house I can't remember quite which one you are you know I really don't live here I'm only visiting. Let him without sinanthropus cast the first Red Guard

and arm him with this closet full of swords.
Enough indeed to start a fencing school if in need of uniforms for
everyone you empty six or seven wards. Edward's unstrung cello
back there in the dark, a stack of primers to initiate the rites on
some Masonic stage. They gave you numbers in the reading room.
You spoke your part as if you were enraged
engaged on every front at once imagine dear your mind become
so like a boil
did you wind the spring of your electric heart.

When does too much of imagine dear become disease.
When does mind become a boil that must lance itself.

Sinanthropus did manage to stand up erect
achieved the use of fire and certain tools for example crudely
        fashioned axe
for example twenty kiloton device exfoliating near Lob Nor he
was discovered circa 1929 at Choukoutien it is not thought
he understood the red shift of Quasars but he lifted up his eyes
but he beheld the sky.

Homology. Homophony. Homeric Hymn.

March northeast to Honan province and display her diaphragm
        your diagram
of all electric circuits at the San Men project
or your relics of the stone age at the San Men gorge. Mercy
        mercy

Madame Mao he'd call out Mother of us all I'd call out mine.

V

The phenomenology of anti-fascist pharmacologists.
The flower in the flame.
The lama whose La Mancha was Lamarckian.

And Mary Quant that year was made an OBE for introducing
miniskirts where fashion plates had illustrated farthingales. You
fell in love. Again. Against your better judgment. Judging from
disasters in your past. You'd pass on tricks conditioned by this new
environment. No pasquinade that year all pas de deux where party
line dissolved in passacaglia the proteins never flowing the right
way. Nonetheless had T. Lshenko risen in the great red dawn to
celebrate inherited callosities among the midwife toads and many
men who since have chosen Cavorject.
Simply self-inject the penis and the medicine will go to work.
Only half of one percent develop Priapism but if you're unlucky,
brother, plan to spend the next three days looking like a randy
faun upon a Grecian urn.

When pharmacologists compounded their phenomena, Omega
dreamed. Alpha held the hands of her ontologist. Pasturage
extended out from Islington to Aldeburgh and you grazed a while
in pastoral relief. Tupping in your tuppence worth of mental astro-
turf you muttered your tu quoque through a proxy in the courts

divorce become an art of divination
in a phase of every trial called discovery.

Aphasia then. And ever afterwards in Asia
world without any end amend.

Printed as required by the Scientologists.

I ask them how much she remembers how much she can under-
stand this execution which on her behalf releases other documents
consents to this Do Not Resuscitate this paper that prohibits inter-
ventions that prohibits both nutrition and hydration but allows

whatever drugs may be obtained to kill the pain ontology a func-
tion of oncology if

protein synthesis and polymeric vectors
mean you are your mother's son your father's fated cowboy
polypeptides flowing like the war

of generations information only out of the nucleic acids Pavlov
buried in a Skinner box with all the roots
of real numbers in a digit that's both decimal and arbitrary.

Tower bridge Falangists drew their falchions if you fell in with the
Trotskyites your politics as puny as falsetto false arrest the agent of
her living will the ticket for Tbilisi in your pocket and Manuel de
Falla blazing at the Proms in Albert Hall.

From Abyssinia to ablative the dosage
is discovered by the dice the delitescent absolute beyond the will

the year run down the tide run out at Tilbury.
She says so Illbeseeinya ram beau   she says

do not resuscitate   do not   let go

Printed in the United States
57574LVS00004B/6